First Try by Greyson

F

How to pass your real estate exam on the first try!

Greyson Roberts

Follow my real estate adventures on YouTube!

Table of Contents

1. Introduction..4
2. What to Expect..7
3. Education Options......................................13
4. Study Hacks..17
5. First Try..22
6. Top 25 vocab words and definitions....................27
7. Top 100 National Practice Questions..................41
8. Conclusion..105

Greyson Roberts

Dedication

I dedicate this book to my loving fiance, Kenzie. I love you more than you could ever comprehend, even though I don't always show it.

First Try

Chapter 1: Introduction

I got my real estate school paid for and passed my exam on the first try within 14 days. You're NEVER going to pass the real estate exam. Furthermore, forget about real estate all together. Did you know that 50% of people who take the real estate exam FAIL on their first attempt? Relish in the harsh reality that you've spent your hard earned cash on a book that essentially scammed you!

Bit by bit, that's most likely what you're agonizingly telling yourself. You feel overwhelmed, like you wasted your money on classes, testing fees and worst of all, you wasted your time. I felt like this even AFTER finishing my national real estate pre-licensing course. It wasn't until after I received my certificate of completion that things truly started to click. Listen, I am not the hottest pot of coffee in the market center,

Greyson Roberts

however, I passed my real estate exam in 14 days, for very little money and on the first try.

Guru after guru, free online test after free online test, blog after blog and video after video. At long last, I understood the questions and answers flew off my tongue. After hearing that my best friend took the test 4 times and another buddy took it *12* times, Yes, TWELVE ($752 in testing fees); I was still extremely nervous. I wanted my real estate license. I want it more than Dave Ramsey wants you to pay off your car loan.

After 3 painstaking hours I finally clicked submit on the delipidated computer mouse provided by the testing center. In 5 short steps I'd receive my answer. I passed. First try. After some time, I have now discovered that real estate is the best business in the world for many, many reasons. Why? It's honestly pretty simple. Everyone on this earth needs a place to live and every business needs a place to operate. If you truly think about it, *everyone* is a potential customer!

I wrote this book to help you (yes, *you*) pass your real estate exam on the first try, quickly and for as little cost as possible.

First Try

Is this an end all be all? No. You will still need to study other sources, not just our 100 of the most common real estate questions or our 25 of the top real estate terms. However, I have provided you with every resource necessary to pass your exam. I don't care who you are, where you're from, if you went to college or not or even your overall level of intellect. If I can do it, trust me, you *certainly* can!

First and foremost, who the hell am I? Now, this isn't an autobiography. With that being said, why would you take advice from me? I am simply a stranger. My name is Greyson Roberts, a Realtor, YouTuber, entrepreneur and now, I guess an author! As I previously mentioned, I went from deciding to get my real estate license all the way to getting my school paid for, taking it all online and passing my exam on the first try. All within 14 days! See, now we're not strangers. Now, listen, this book is straight to the point, informal and lighthearted. Bear with me to the end as I will get you on your way to making lots of money. So, let's get started!

Greyson Roberts

Chapter 2: What to Expect

Precisely how I got into real estate is beyond the scope of this book. Long story short, I scheduled a meeting with a top producing real estate agent in the area with my goal being to tour his luxury listing for my YouTube channel. The meeting took an unexpected turn, and by the end, I decided to pursue my true passion of real estate and committed to getting my license. I went from that initial meeting to smashing through my online courses and getting my license all in 14 days. Best of all, I passed my test on the first try!

We will talk about this agent and current day mentor later in this book. However, for now, it's important to understand how little I knew about the journey ahead. That journey being, getting my real estate license as soon as possible with the least amount of money. As you probably noticed, that's what this book is all about!

First Try

My goal is for you to replicate my real estate exam test success. From that initial meeting all the way to test day, I was extremely anxious. I'm sure you feel the same way. Let me put your mind at ease. It's not as hard as you think! It seems overwhelming to everybody at first but coming out successfully on the other side with a literal license to print money was not as daunting in hindsight. Do. Not. Worry. It's cake!

Now, it's important to understand that there are essentially two tests you'll be taking. The national and the state. Every state portion of the real estate exam is unique to where you live. Since I can't cover every state in this book our focus will be primarily on the national exam. This is the biggest, scariest and most difficult of the two. Let's discuss the steps involved in getting your real estate license, using my home state Missouri as the state example throughout the duration of this book. This may look a little different depending on where you're from and the time you're reading this book. Here's the gist of it.

- Take the 48 hour national pre-licensing course

Greyson Roberts

- Pass the 48 hour national pre-licensing exam
- Take the 24 hour state practice course
- Pass the 24 hour state practice course
- Receive your course completion certificates and schedule your exam
- Study, study and study!
- Successfully pass your real exam on the *first try*
- Call whatever brokerage you'd like to join and discuss your next steps to onboarding

That's it! That's all you need to do to get licensed. Now, let's look at the costs. These numbers will vary depending on which school you go to, whether it's online or in-person, if you join NAR (National Association of Realtors), state requirements, etc. Here were MY costs, which may be similar to yours.

- 48 hour & 24 hour pre-licensing course - $350 (or free)
- National and state exam - $62
- Fingerprinting - $40
- National & local realtor dues - $1,200 (prorated)

First Try

Now, there are more or less costs involved. You'll want access to the MLS and whatever lockbox system you use in your local market. Here in southwest Missouri, we use the Supra eKey system. The unit itself cost me $120, activation fee $40 and a $15/mo recurring charge. You may not find it necessary to join your national and local board of Realtors, however, I highly suggest it. They offer great training, resources and a powerful brand name. If the cost is too high for you (which I completely understand) you can always join later after your first closing. Finances in the real estate business is a topic for another book.

So those are the costs. What about the course itself? Both courses will take you through units, most likely with each unit having a short quiz at the end. When you first begin the 48 hour national course, you're quickly going to realize that you don't even know what you don't know. I remember my first 30 minutes into the course. It seemed like a foreign language and I immediately doubted myself. You will likely experience the same thing. Again, *don't worry*. Everyone feels this way. With the methods used throughout this book, a potato could pass their real estate exam.

Greyson Roberts

We will get to the course success and study tips momentarily. For now, let's keep digging into what to expect. You should expect to feel overwhelmed. You will fail quiz after quiz. It took me 3 tries to pass the final 48 hour course exam! Just know, things only started to click for me AFTER both the 48 and 24 hour courses were completed. It was what I did in between course completion and exam day that truly made test day successful. Let me say that again. *It's what I did in between course completion and exam day that mattered the most.*

One last piece of advice regarding expectations. You realistically won't use 80% of the information you will learn in these courses. They are designed to help you pass a test, NOT help you become a successful agent. That's a story for another day. However, you must know all the concepts presented in the course material for the sake of getting that little piece of paper that says you're legit. Let's talk about some pre-licensing education options and how you can potentially get your real estate school for 100% free. And no, not by waving an unregistered firearm in the real estate

First Try

commissions office! Well, now that I mention it, that may work (joke, of course).

Chapter 3: Education Options

You may be asking yourself, where do I even find an approved pre-licensing course? There's actually many options depending on your location and if you choose to go online or in person. My courses were online with the national and state often coming bundled together as one. Make sure whatever you pick will actually be accepted by the real estate commission. If not, you'll have wasted your time and money for nothing. Luckily, I've got a couple recommendations!

My specific course was actually free. Yes, *free*! Now, I can't say this will work for you, but here's how I got my school completely paid for. My local Keller Williams market center hosts a new agent career seminar every Friday at noon. This seminar lasts about an hour and the seminar host runs you

First Try

through a slide show basically selling you on Keller Williams. They explain why becoming an agent is a phenomenal career and, of course, why you should join their brokerage. At the end of the presentation, they offered to pay for my online school! Why? Well, I can only assume that if they offered to pay, I'd have no reason not to get my license and join Keller Williams. Needless to say, it worked. Luckily, I absolutely love Keller Williams! I recently attended a second seminar with my buddy who will be joining my real estate company, BOSS Properties. Once again, I confirmed that this is a national thing, not just a lucky break on my part.

Keep in mind, this may not work for you. Call your local KW and ask if they host a career seminar. If so, go! It's a great presentation that will answer every question you may have and they may even pay for your online courses like they did mine! The education provider they partner with is called Kaplan. You can simply look them up and enroll yourself for about $350. Here's why I recommend Kaplan. It's hard! It comes with over 1,000 customizable quiz questions that are more difficult than the exam. In fact, once I took my actual exam, I thought it was way easier! This is a great thing. Plus,

Greyson Roberts

they have videos. Finally, did I mention it's *FREE*? That's my favorite price.

The second best choice is realestateexpress.com. I know many agents who went through this online course. They have packages as low as $160! Although, real estate express is *100% reading*. Kaplans state portion was all *video*. Personally, video helped me understand the concepts being provided MUCH easier. There are lots of great options so be sure to see what online schools are approved in your state.

You can also attend in-person classes. They will move much faster but it just depends on what you think will be best for you. I know 2 agents who both paid a premium for 8 full days of in-person training. Agent 1 took four attempts to pass the exam and agent 2 took the exam 12 times. Yes, TWELVE. Remember what I said about the courses not setting you up for success in real estate sales but rather to help you pass the exam? Well, both agents 1 and 2 are amazing Realtors: It doesn't matter how many times you retake the real estate exam. You only truly fail when you throw in the towel.

First Try

I've been talking a big game about how easy the exam is to pass. I know what you're thinking, what a douche canoe! Well, it's easy if you truly prepare yourself. By the end of this book, you'll know exactly how to do that. What if you don't pass it on the first try? Tough shit! Get back on the horse cowboy, we've got money to make. Shake it off and give 'er another go. No biggy.

Greyson Roberts

Chapter 4: Study Hacks

Hands down, this is the most important chapter in this whole book. Arguably, the next chapter will be the second most impactful to your first try success. There are countless websites, free quizzes, YouTube channels and info products out there all with the goal of helping you pass your exam. If you're like me, you don't want to sift through thousands of links in order to maybe stumble upon something that will help.

The worst part is, you won't know what's good study material and what's not because you haven't seen the test! Many of the study tools out there will simply waste your time and give you false confidence walking into the exam. I've compiled every category I could think of and will straight up tell you the specific study materials I think contributed the MOST to my success on the real estate exam. All study tools are not created equal. Some free exams are easy on purpose to build

First Try

your confidence so you pay for the whole thing. Here's the truth.

Pre-licensing course practice tests

Hands down, the practice quizzes your online course providers give you are my favorite. I took 500 practice quizzes from my Kaplan course. Think about it, if you're spending hundreds of dollars on state approved pre-licensing education, they better be good! If you spent all that money, ran through the course materials, utilized their practice tests and it didn't actually help you pass the exam, they'd go out of business! You get what you pay for. Free tests on Google are alright, however, they're easy and the quiz questions are much easier. Most of the free tests offer an option to pay the site to unlock "full practice exams". You already paid for the best, hardest and most in depth practice quizzes on the market. I know for a fact that Kaplan quizzes are *harder* than the exam. Again, that's a wonderful thing.

Generic online tests

You've probably Googled: "free real estate practice test". I sure did! I took every free test on the first two pages of Google.

Now, these tests certainly don't hurt. I also don't consider them a waste of time per se. Like I said, they're usually much easier and very short, unless you pay a premium for the full experience. I don't recommend paying for any online practice exams. You can take plenty of short and free versions. I only recommend spending time on free online tests if you ran through all the quizzes provided in your pre-licensing course. Generic online tests rank low on the totem pole of study tools.

Flashcards

I love flashcards! Don't waste your time creating them by hand. I hear this far too often. No thanks, boomers! Simply type into Google: "nation real estate exam quizlet". You'll find hundreds of amazing made-for-you practice questions with the answer on the "back" of quizlet's digital flashcards. These are great, however where the Quizlet format truly shines is utilizing the site to memorize real estate vocab. Big, big tip. Memorize the vocab! If you simply understand what every word in the questions means, the process of elimination will carry you to the correct answer. We will talk more about this in the next chapter. Vocab, vocab and more vocab!

First Try

YouTube

There are literally thousands of YouTube videos and podcasts running through sample questions. Now, honestly I didn't find as much value in this type of content. Trust me, I love YouTube. I have 5 income producing YouTube channels! However, when I was studying for my exam, I became a sponge. Soaking up every bit of real estate information as humanly possible! Since I don't condone reading and driving, I resorted to playing YouTube videos in my car. This ended up being pretty awesome! Made my commutes more entertaining and I was learning a lot! However, the people who host these video tests often spend too much time off topic. I noticed it could be *5 minutes* in between questions. This made these videos extremely frustrating at times. I only recommend watching/listening to YouTube videos and podcasts if you're driving or working on something else. If you are going to try out these videos, I've found that one channel hands down does it best. Prep Agent on YouTube is who provided the most value to me on my commutes. Don't waste your time on any other channel. They're the real deal!

Greyson Roberts

Long story short, I highly recommend spending most of your study time focused on your main course providers quizzes and utilizing quizlet to rapidly memorize vocab. There will be a strange period in between receiving your course completion certificate and your scheduled exam day. For me, this window was 4 days. Talk about the longest 4 days of my life! Take advantage of this lul by cramming as many sample questions as possible. This time is absolutely the most crucial to your first real estate exam success. This 4 day window is where the concepts truly started sticking in my brain more than they ever did in all 72 hours of my pre-licensing course.

Chapter 5: First Try

Everyone's goal is to pass the real estate exam on the first try. It's a 4 hour test, costs money and causes a lot of unnecessary stress. Not to mention, you want to dive head-first into the best business on the planet! So, why is it that 50% of people who take the real estate exam fail on their first attempt? Well, by design, they don't know what to expect. You can't cheat on the real estate exam, therefore you truly need to know the answer to 70% of the questions to pass. Is the test really that hard? Simply, no. The real estate exam is NOT hard. However, you're probably brand new to the industry and are essentially starting from ground zero.

The real estate exam is detailed and WILL try to trick you. Most people who take the test only prepare themselves by completing the pre-licensing course. Remember when I said the most important time is between course completion and test day? That's 100% true. That's when you get to take hard

Greyson Roberts

practice quizzes and focus on complicated vocab to truly push your understanding of the concepts. Most people don't think they need to continue studying. Why would you? My course was 72 hours and I passed both course exams. Shouldn't I be more than prepared?

No, no and no. The real estate exam is not hard, but it *is* complicated and long. It's literally impossible to try and memorize the questions without understanding the concepts. Why can't I just memorize the questions? Simply because every test is randomized and unique. You won't take the same test twice. I made the MAJOR mistake of trying to memorize the specific questions without understanding the answer. DO NOT DO THIS. Like I said, your real exam will be randomized! No website has the exact exam questions. If a website claims they do have the exact questions, they're either lying or breaking the law. Please, do not make this mistake I and most other people make. Luckily, I caught myself doing this early enough to implement the tactics I used to pass my exam on the first try. NEVER try to memorize the answers to specific questions. You must....

First Try

Understand the concepts

I can not emphasize this enough. UNDERSTAND THE QUESTION YOU'RE ANSWERING. If you come across a question asking about an easement and you don't understand what an easement truly is, STOP. Stop and research what is an easement, how it's used and why it's used. If you understand the concept of an easement, you'll be able to answer ANY question regarding easements without having to guess or try to memorize that specific question that will not be on your real exam. At first, this will take more time to get through questions. Over time, you'll read questions and know every single word definition by heart!

If you see a question asking what is an addendum, make sure you know the difference between an addendum and amendment. Understanding the concept of both vocab terms will help you navigate questions with similar sounding answers. What about the difference between an encroachment and an encumbrance? It's all too easy to walk into your testing center and quickly realize you don't truly understand the concepts. Okay, you know the definition of earnest money. That's awesome, you MUST know the definition of earnest money. However, *when and why* does earnest money make sense? The real estate exam likes to throw in long and over worded questions. They're not going to ask, what is a contingency? It's more likely to ask something like this:

Buyer Jim offers $178k, $5k over asking. Seller Joe accepts Jim's offer and they go under contract. Jim discovers a hole in the roof during the due diligence phase and wants to back out of the contract. What contingency must Jim have included in the sales contract in order to back out of the deal while protecting his earnest money?

a. Roof contingency
b. Repair contingency
c. Encumbrance contingency
d. Inspection contingency

This is exactly how the real estate exam works. The sooner you realize this the sooner you can adjust your studying. Oh, in case you're wondering, the answer is D. If you understood

First Try

the concepts of contingency, you'd know the answer halfway through the question without even looking at the answer options. This is the point I am trying to make. *Understand the concepts*, don't just memorize random questions.

The second biggest factor playing into your first try success is understanding vocab. You may know what a leasehold estate is, but if you can't define it, you'll miss too many questions. There are a LOT of vocab definition questions and understanding these will make you sound like a pro on your first day being a real estate agent. I will be providing 25 of the most commonly used vocab terms along with 100 common questions asked on the real estate exam. Quizlet is hands down the best way to memorize hundreds of definitions fast and for free.

You may be wondering how much time you need to dedicate to studying. I dedicated literally 80% of my free time to studying! That's most of every single day! Keep in mind you MUST become a sponge starting the day you enroll in real estate school all the way to passing your exam on the first

Greyson Roberts

try. Remember, this helps you pass the test the quickest and for the least amount of money.

First Try

Chapter 6: Top 25 vocab words and definitions

Here are 25 of the most important real estate vocab terms you will need to know in order to pass your real estate exam on the first try. I highly recommend you pick up a copy of the book " Dictionary of Real Estate Term". I picked up my copy for $4 with free shipping on ebay. This is a 600 page dictionary of real estate specific terms. This is a great resource to have in your day-to-day real estate practice. In fact, that's exactly where I sourced these definitions from. As for study purposes, don't forget to utilize all the hard work some nameless sole spent compiling digital vocab flashcards!

1. Addendum - something added, as an attachment to a contract. Same as a rider.
    a. Example: An addendum to the contract of a sale described the type of financing that the

buyer must secure to be required to purchase the property.

2. Agency Disclosure - a written explanation, to be signed by a prospective buyer or seller, explaining to the client the role that the broker plays in the transaction. The purpose of disclosure is to explain whether the broker represents the buyer or seller or is a dual agent (representing both) or a subagent (an agent of the seller's broker). This allows the customer to understand to which party the broker owes loyalty.

   a. Example: The agency disclosure agreement submitted by Bob Broker to the prospective buyer for his signature states that Bob Broker is a subagent of the seller's agent and will be paid by the sling broker. This puts the buyer on notice that Bob Broker's loyalty is to the seller. Without the disclosure, the prospective buyer might have mistakenly thought that Bob Broker was working for him.

First Try

3. Amendment - change, correction, or extension of an agreement that does not modify the basic thrust of the agreement.
    a. Example: Lease amendments were used to:
        i. Renew the lease for an additional term
        ii. Change the percentage rent requirement
        iii. Clarify the tenants defined parking area

4. Amortized Loan - any loan with at least some payments to principal
    a. Example: A loan of $10,000 at 10% interest requires annual payments of $1,200. Because the payments exceed the interest required, the loan balance will be reduced, so it is an amortized loan. Contrast with interest-only loans.

5. Blockbusting - a racially discriminatory and illegal practice of coercing a party to sell a home to someone of a minority race or ethnic backgournd, then using scare tactics to cause others in the neighborhood and informing them that their property's value will fall if they don't sell right away at a depressed offered price.
    a. Example: A sales agent arranges a sale in which a minority family entered a previously all-white neighborhood. The agent then engages in blockbusting by contacting other owners in the neighborhood and informing them that their property's value will fall if they don't sell right away at a depressed offered price.

6. Contingency - a clause in a purchase agreement specifying an action or requirement that must be met for the contract to become legally binding.
    a. Example: The buyer pulled out of a sales contract while keeping his earnest money

First Try

   due to his financing contingency being in place.

7. Deed - a written document, properly signed and delivered, that conveys title to real property.
   a. Example: In exchange for the agreed upon terms of a contract, including the purchase price, at closing the seller delivers a deed to the buyer.

8. Disclosure Statement - a statement required by law, in which sellers of particular kinds of property, or under certain circumstances, must reveal specific information to potential buyers.
   a. Examples: Most states require sellers of real estate to disclose any "dangerous condition" to potential buyers
   b. Many sellers of investment interests in real estate are required to disclose their own interest and even profit potential
   c. Sellers of time-share interests must disclose which portions of the project will be retained

by the developer, and the costs and conditions of use by time-share buyers.

9. Due Diligence - making a reasonable effort to provide accurate, complete information. A study that often precedes the purchase of property, which is the property and expected investment performance; the underwriting of a loan or investment.
   a. Example: The pension fund sent various experts to perform a due diligence study of a property it was considering for purchase. Matters to be considered included the mechanical and electrical systems of the building, local market conditions and competition for the property, and environmental hazards.

10. Earnest Money - a deposit made by a purchaser of real estate to evidence good faith.
    a. Example: It is customary for the buyer to give the seller earnest money at the time a sales contract is signed. The earnest money

First Try

generally is credited to the down payment at closing. Until closing a broker must hold earnest money in a separate account.

11. Easement - the right, privilege, or interest that one party has in the land of another.
    a. Example: The right of public utility companies to lay their lines across others' property is a utility easement.

12. Encroachment - a building, a part of a building, or an obstruction that physically intrudes upon, overlaps, or trespasses upon the property of another.
    a. Example: A part of the building on lot A is an encroachment on lot B. This situation probably occurred because of a faulty survey of lot A.

13. Encumbrance - any right to or interest in land that affects its value. Includes outstanding mortgage loans, unpaid taxes, easements, deed restrictions.

a. Example: Encumbrances on blackacres include 3 mortgages, 4 leases, a mechanics lien, and a deed restriction preventing the sale of alcoholic beverages on the land.

14. Leasehold -An interest in real estate characterized by the right to possess and use, but not actual ownership.
    a. Example: Mason possesses a long-term lease on a property. She may obtain a loan with the leasehold pledged as collateral. If the contract rent required by the lease is lower than market rents. Mason's leasehold will have a positive value.

15. Legal description - legally acceptable identification of real estate by one of the following:
    a. The government rectangular survey
    b. Metes and bounds
    c. Recorded plat (lot and block number)

i. Example: the seller was required to include a legal description in the deed.

16. Lien - a charge against property making it security for the payment of a debt, judgment, mortgage, or taxes; it is a type of encumbrance. A specific lien is against certain property only. A general lien is against all of the property owned by the debtor
    a. Example: Abel failed to pay the contractor for work performed on his home. The contractor filed a mechanics lien against the property for the amount due.

17. Marketable Title - a title so free from defect that a court will enforce the title's acceptance by a purchaser. Contrast with cloud on the title.
    a. Example: Through a divorce settlement, Collins obtained certain ownership rights to a property. She now wishes to sell the property. To obtain a marketable title, she must obtain a quitclaim deed from her

former husband, thereby curing a defect in her title.

18. Real Estate - Land and everything more or less attached to it. Ownership below to the center of the earth and above to the heavens. Distinguished from personal property. Same as realty.

19. Refinance - to replace an old loan(s) with a new loan(s).
    a. Example: Garner has a $30,000 loan against her house, which is worth $200,000. She desires cash to pay for a college education. By refinancing the home with a new $150,000 loan, she will realize $114,000 in cash after paying $5,000 in transaction costs.

20. Rehab - to restore a structure to condition of good repair.
    a. Example: An old building has deteriorated to the point of prohibiting profitable operation. The owner faces the choice of demolition of

First Try

the structure and rebuilding or rehabilitation to restore the building to a competitive position.

21. Severalty - the ownership of real property by an individual as an individual.
    a. Example: The owner enjoys working the land without partners in its ownership.

22. Special Assessment - an assessment made against a property to pay for a public/ private improvement by which the assessed property is supposed to be especially benefited.
    a. Example: The Lawson's own a house in a developing section of the city. When the city constructs curbs and gutters along their street, the Lawsons are levied a special assessment, in the form of a one-time tax, to pay for the construction.

23. Title - evidence that the owner of land is in lawful possession thereof; evidence of ownership. See also adverse possession, certificate of title, clear title, cloud on the title, marketable title.
    a. Example: Title to land does not merely imply that a person has the right of possession, because one may have the right to possession and have no title. Title does ordinarily signify rights to possession in addition to evidence of ownership.

24. Write-Off - an accounting procedure where an asset whose value has declined is reserved or taken off the books.
    a. Example: To certify a financial statement, the CPA insisted that uncollected rents from the previous year be entirely written off, as the possibility of collection was minimal.

25. Zoning - a legal mechanism for local governments to regulate the use of privately owned real property by specific application of police power to prevent

First Try

conflicting land uses and promote orderly development. All privately owned land within the jurisdiction is placed within designated zones that limit the type and intensity of development permitted.

    a. Example: Before a tract of land may be developed, the intended use must be permitted under the existing zoning classification. If the proposed use is not permitted, the developer must apply for an amendment to the zoning ordinance, or for rezoning. Such amendments are granted by the local governing body, generally following a public hearing and recommendation from the planning commission.

Greyson Roberts

Chapter 7: 100 of the Most Common Real Estate Exam Questions

Here are 100 of the most common and basic questions you're likely to encounter on the real estate exam. Keep in mind these questions are not the exact questions on the exam! Otherwise, I'm pretty sure I'd be in jail (free rent). These questions are also in my opinion some of the *easiest* questions you'll likely face. I know for a fact that Kaplan and legit exam questions are longer, more intricate and detailed . These sample questions are the same concepts, with more wording to complicate and throw you off. These questions I've compiled are simply designed to get you started understanding *concepts*. You won't be able to answer these by simply reading this book. No way! However, you can turn to

First Try

this as a guide to track your progress as you go throughout your course and study materials. Don't take your exam until you can answer every single one of these questions with ease!

Property Ownership

1. An owner of real property conveys a life estate to her granddaughter and stipulates that on her death the estate will pass to her daughter-in-law. The daughter-in-law has which of the following
    a. Legal life estate
    b. Estate for years
    c. Residential sales contract
    d. Remainder interest

Answer: a. Remainder interest

Explanation: The owner's death will end the life estate conveyed to her granddaughter, which will then mean the holder of the remainder interest, the daughter-in-law, will have fee simple absolute ownership of the property. An estate for years is a leasehold estate that continues for any definite period. A legal life estate is a freehold estate created out of a reservation.

2. What is considered the least specific method for identifying a legal description?
    a. Street address
    b. Metes and bounds
    c. Survey
    d. Tax records

Answer: a. Street address

Explanation: A street address is not a legal description and, therefore, not as precise.

3. An owner of real property tells his next-door neighbor that he can store his camper in his yard for a few months until he needs the space. The property owner does not charge the neighbor any rent for the use of his yard. The owner has given his neighbor
    a. Easement by prescription

First Try

      b.   Estate for years
      c.   Easement by necessity
      d.   A license

Answer: d. A license

Explanation: A license is a revocable personal privilege to use the land of another for a specific purpose, and the right is given orally or informally

4. A junior lien may become first in priority if the original lender agrees to execute
      a.   A deed of trust
      b.   A lien release
      c.   A subordination agreement
      d.   A second mortgage agreement

Answer: a. A subordination agreement

Explanation: If the original lender signs a subordination agreement, another loan assigned more later may be allowed to take first place and the original loan to second place. A deed of trust is a third-party instrument in which the deed is given as security for the loan to a third party, the trustee. A second mortgage agreement binds a borrower to repay a loan taken on a property on which the borrower already has a first mortgage.

5. All are fixtures EXCEPT
    a. An oven built into the cabinetry
    b. A refrigerator installed into the cupboard
    c. Prized rose bushes
    d. A freestanding refrigerator

Answer: d. A freestanding refrigerator

Explanation: The answer is a freestanding refrigerator. Fixtures are determined by attachment, adaptation, and agreement. A microwave plugged into the wall is personal property.

6. How do you transfer the ownership of real property?
    a. Bill of sale
    b. Deed
    c. Title

First Try

       d.   Pinky promise

Answer: b. Deed

Explanation: A deed is used to transfer ownership of real property.

7. An owner of real property who has complete control is said to own

    a.   An Estate for years
    b.   A Periodic estate
    c.   A fee simple absolute
    d.   A defeasible fee estate

Answer: c. A fee simple absolute

Explanation: The highest interest in real estate recognized by law is the fee simple or fee simple absolute estate, in which the holder is entitled to all rights of the property.

8. How many acres are in a section in a rectangular survey?

    a.   120

    b.   160

    c.   240

    d.   640

Answer: d. 640

Explanation: There are 640 acres in a "section".

9. There has been a lien placed against specific properties that benefit from public improvement. What is this?
    a. Tax assessment
    b. A special assessment
    c. Mortgage lien
    d. Tax lien

Answer: b. Special assessment

Explanation: Special assessments are taxes levied on real estate to fund improvements beneficial to the property. The specific improvements are paid for by the special assessments.

First Try

10. How will a corporation take title to real property?
    a. Tenants in common
    b. Tenants in severalty
    c. Join tenants
    d. Severalty

Answer: d. Severalty

Explanation: A corporation is legally treated as a single person and may own property in severalty. A corporation is an artificial person in the eyes of the law.

11. All of these will place a lien on a property EXCEPT
    a. Unpaid contractor bill
    b. Unpaid mortgage
    c. An encroachment
    d. Unpaid property taxes

Answer: c. An encroachment

Greyson Roberts

Explanation: A lien is placed on real property when you owe money related to the property. Debtors can collect their debts upon the sale of your home.

12. Which term refers to sole ownership in real property?
    a. Fee simple absolute
    b. Join tenancy
    c. Severalty
    d. Tenancy by the entirety

Answer: c. Severalty

Explanation: Severalty ownership is ownership by one person severed and cut off from all others. Tenancy in common and joint tenancy are forms of joint ownership. Tenancy by the entirety is personal or real property belonging to spouses according to state laws.

13. If you have the legal right to cross over your neighbor's land to get to your house, what is in place?
    a. An encroachment

First Try

      b. An easement

      c. A license

      d. Permission

Answer: b. An easement

Explanation: An easement is a right of use or passage and is not an encroachment.

14. A mechanics lien can hinder the sale of a property because

      a. There is an encumbrance

      b. There is an easement

      c. There is an encroachment

      d. There is a judgment

Answer: a. There is an encumbrance

Explanation: An encumbrance is a claim, charge, or liability that attaches to real estate.

15. Which lien is voluntary?

Greyson Roberts

    a. Tax lien
    b. Mechanics lien
    c. Judgment lien
    d. Mortgage lien

Answer: d. Mortgage lien

Explanation: You're volunteering to take on a mortgage on your own free will.

Land Use

16. John has operated a barber shop in a neighborhood for the last 34 years. John's store is the only retail property in the area that is zoned residential. What is John's barber shop an example of?
    a. Breaking the law
    b. Nonconforming use
    c. Variance of the zoning laws
    d. Violation of zoning laws

Answer: b. Nonconforming use

First Try

Answer: Nonconforming use is the legal use of a property that existed before the current zoning ordinances took place but no longer conform to current zoning laws.

17. Which of the following can a homeowners association control the number of?
    a. Age of residence in the neighborhood (not 55+)
    b. Ethnic groups allowed
    c. Pets allowed
    d. Children allowed

Answer: c. Pets allowed
Explanation: HOA can NEVER impose restrictions that would violate any federal fair housing laws.

18. What is the point of zoning ordinances?
    a. Flex the policing power of the city
    b. Limit the number of ethnic groups

    c.   Protect neighborhoods from commercial encroachment
    d.   Confirm land use conforms to the master plan

Answer: d. Confirm land use conforms to the master plan
Explanation: Zoning ordinances are the local laws implemented to make sure proposed land use confirms the cities overall goals of growth.

19. What must a homeowner do before constructing an additional bathroom to their home?
    a.   Apply for a building permit
    b.   Ask the city mayor for permission
    c.   Get a certificate of occupancy
    d.   Receive a code certificate

Answer: a. Apply for a building permit
Explanation: Before the homeowner begins construction on any home additions, they must apply and receive a building permit.

First Try

20. What is an eminent domain example of?
    a. Assessment
    b. Involuntary alienation
    c. Voluntary alienation
    d. Escheat

Answer: b. Involuntary alienation

Explanation: Involuntary alienation occurs when property is transferred without the owner's consent.

Financing

21. Which mortgage type does a borrower only pay interest for a stated period of time and pays off the principal at the end of the term?
    a. Wraparound loan
    b. Balloon loan
    c. Residential Loan
    d. Interest-only loan

Answer: d. Interest-only loan

Explanation: Interest-only mortgages require payment of interest only for a stated period of time, with the principal balance and interest recalculated over the remaining years of the loan interest-only loan.

22. Which clause in a mortgage would make the balance due when a homeowner sells their home and acquires a new loan?
    a. Acceleration clause
    b. Due-on-sale clause
    c. Home sale clause
    d. Mortgage release clause

Answer: b. Due-on-sale clause

Explanation: A due-on-sale clause is what comes into effect if real property is sold. The lender may declare the entire debt due upon sale.

First Try

23. Which type of property qualifies for an FHA loan?
    a. Commercial
    b. Industrial
    c. 5 unit non owner-occupied multifamily complex
    d. 1-4 unit owner-occupied multifamily complex

Answer: d. 1-4 unit owner-occupied multifamily complex.
Explanation: FHA is a type of residential loan. FHA requires the owner must live in the property for at least 1 year.

24. A client asks you a question regarding financing options. How should you respond?
    a. Answer their question ASAP
    b. Suggest they talk to a CPA
    c. Suggest they speak with an attorney
    d. Suggest they speak with a lending professional

Answer: d. Suggest they speak with a lending professional

Explanation: Real estate professionals are not permitted to give financial, legal or tax advice. You must refer your client to the appropriate professional.

25. Which law determines the maximum interest rate a lender can charge?
    a. Truth-in-lending laws
    b. Borrower protection laws
    c. Usury Laws
    d. Blockbusting

Answer: c. Usury Laws

Explanation: Usury is the act of charging an interest rate in excess of limits permitted by law.

26. Which property requires a commercial loan?
    a. Non-owner occupied single family home
    b. A fourplex
    c. A fiveplex
    d. A duplex

First Try

Answer: c. A fiveplex

Explanation: 1-4 units are considered residential, 5 or more is considered residential commercial.

27. Which statement BEST describes equity?
    a. Outstanding mortgage balance
    b. Current market value
    c. Current market value minus property debt
    d. Amount of loan balance paid down

Answer: c. Current market value minus property debt

Explanation: Equity is the current market value of a property minus the balance of the loan.

Agency

28. What is puffing?
    a. Exaggeration of a properties benefits

b. Misrepresentation of a property

c. Fraud

d. Misrepresenting financials of an income producing property

Answer: a. Exaggeration of a properties benefits

Explanation: Puffing is not illegal unlike misrepresentation. An example of puffing is as follows, "this house has the best view in the neighborhood".

29. What is dual agency?
    a. When an agent purchases their own property
    b. When a broker purchases their own property
    c. When a broker/agent sells their own property
    d. When a broker/agent represents both buyer and seller

Answer: d. When a broker/agent represents both buyer and seller

First Try

Explanation: Dual agency occurs when you are representing both the buyer and seller side of a real estate transaction.

30. What is the contract that secures the employment of a brokerage firm to find an able buyer for a seller?
    a. Residential sales contract
    b. Sale contract
    c. Listing contract
    d. Buyer representation agreement

Answer: c. Listing contract

Explanation: A Listing contract is an employment agreement of a brokerage firm to find a ready, willing and able buyer for a seller.

31. What should an agent do if they discover a prospect already has an agent agreement in place at an open house?
    a. Require that they sign a representation agreement with you

b. Still provide the open house but do not try to get them to switch agents
c. Offer to help them buy another home
d. Discover more information about the agency representation agreement

Answer: Still provide the open house but do not try to get them to switch agents.

Explanation: If you discover a prospect already has a representation agreement in place with another agent, you can not allow them to employ you.

32. A prospect starts disclosing financial and personal information. What should you do?
    a. Require them to sign a representation agreement
    b. Tell them to talk to a CPA
    c. Provide your services as normal
    d. Ignore them

Answer: a. Require them to sign a representation agreement

First Try

Explanation: If a prospect begins to disclose financial and/or personal information to you, require them to officially hire you as their agent.

33. A listing broker is typically which of the following?
    a. Dual agent
    b. General agent
    c. Universal agent
    d. Special agent

Answer: d. Special agent

Explanation: A broker is typically a special agent authorized to represent the client in one specific real estate translation, with no power to bind the client.

34. Which contract secures a brokerage firm to help a buyer in finding a suitable property to buy?
    a. Residential sales contract
    b. Buyer representation agreement
    c. Listing agreement

d.   Broker disclosure form

Answer: b. Buyer representation agreement

Explanation: A buyer representation agreement is a contract of employment in which the broker is employed as the buyer's agent in finding a suitable property.

Property disclosures

35. Information that would be considered import to a buyer in making the decision to purchase a piece of property is known as
    a. Physical defect
    b. Material fact
    c. Latent defect
    d. Inspection report

Answer: b. Material fact

Explanation: A material fact is any known fact about a property that would influence a buyer's purchasing decision.

First Try

36. What disclosure applies *specifically* to every home built before 1978?
    a. Sellers disclosure
    b. Asbestos disclosure
    c. Lead-based paint disclosure
    d. Mold disclosure

Answer: c. Lead-based paint disclosure

Explanation: Homes built before 1978 commonly used lead-based paint. This kind of paint has been deemed too dangerous for modern day use and must be disclosed.

37. Hidden defects that are not immediately obvious in a property are known as
    a. Latent defects
    b. Material defects
    c. Latent facts
    d. Material facts

Answer: a. Latent defects

Greyson Roberts

Explanation: A material fact is issues with a property in which are more obvious, hidden issues that are not obvious are known as a latent defect.

38. When are disclosure forms usually presented to the buyer?
    a. After an offer is made
    b. Before an offer is made
    c. At an agreed upon time between the buyer and seller
    d. At closing

Answer: b. Before an offer is made
Explanation: Disclosures should always be presented to a buyer BEFORE an offer is made. Disclosures may help a buyer decide if they want to place an offer on a property or not.

39. Property that is associated with a bad event, such as death, is known as
    a. A dangerous property

First Try

      b. A defeasible property

      c. A disclosed property

      d. A stigmatized property

Answer: d. A stigmatized property

Explanation: A stigmatized property is a property that was the site of a suicide, murder or other undesireable events of the like.

Contracts

40. If a minor signs a sales contract, the contract is
    a. Voidable by the seller
    b. Void
    c. Voidable by the minor
    d. Valid

Answer: c. Voidable by the minor

Explanation: Minors who are parties to a contract always make the contract voidable. It is incumbent upon the seller to not allow a minor to enter into a contract. The seller will have to wait for the minor to cancel or move forward.

41. A contract that has yet to be performed is
    a. Void
    b. In escrow
    c. Executory
    d. Pending

Answer: c. Executory

Explanation: A contract that has not yet been fully performed is executory.

42. Electronic signatures are considered
    a. As legally binding as ink signatures
    b. Voidable
    c. Not legally binding
    d. Temporary, only valid for 30 days until replaced with ink

First Try

Answer: a. As legally binding as ink signatures

Explanation: E-signatures are just as legally binding as ink. Electronic signatures are commonplace in modern real estate practice.

43. A type of listing illegal in some states where the listing agent receives any amount over the agreed upon listing price is know as a
    a. Illegal listing
    b. Voidable listing
    c. Net listing
    d. Gross listing

Answer: c. Net listing

Explanation: A net listing is a type of listing in which an owner sets a certain amount of money that they want to receive from the sale of their home. Any dollar amount over their set price will go straight to the broker. This is illegal in many states.

44. A buyer and seller enter into a contract in which the buyer gets to pull out of the contract and protect his earnest money if he doesn't secure financing. This clause in a sales contract is known as

    a. A voidable contract
    b. An encumbrance
    c. A financing contingency
    d. A disclosure

Answer: c. A financing contingency

Explanation: In real estate, a contingency refers to a clause in a purchase agreement specifying an action or requirement that must be met for the contract to become legally binding. Both the buyer and seller must agree to the terms of each contingency and sign the contract before it becomes binding.

45. If upon receipt of an offer to purchase John's property, the seller makes a counteroffer, the original offer is considered as

    a. Voidable
    b. Contingent

First Try

      c. Valid
      d. Terminated

Answer: d. Terminated

Explanation: Once a counteroffer is presented and accepted, the original offer is considered terminated.

46. Under the statute of frauds, all contracts for the sale of real property must
    a. Be in writing to be enforceable
    b. Be legible
    c. Accompany earnest money
    d. Created by a broker

Answer: a. Be in writing to be enforceable

Explanation: The statute of frauds states for real estate sales contracts to be in writing to be enforceable.

47. In the event an offer from a buyer is accepted by the seller, what kind of title does the buyer hold?
    a. None

    b. Escrow

    c. Equitable

    d. Full

Answer: c. Equitable

Explanation: The seller holds legal title until closing, the buyer holds equitable title.

Transfer of title

48. Title to real property passes when a valid deed is
    a. Signed and recorded
    b. Signed and notarized
    c. Accepted
    d. Delivered and accepted

Answer: d. Delivered and accepted

Explanation: Title to real property is not considered transferred until officially delivered and accepted.

First Try

49. Which of the following is considered voluntary alienation?
    a. The sale of a property
    b. Condemnation
    c. Adverse possession
    d. Foreclosure

Answer: a. The sale of a property
Explanation: Voluntary alienation is when the owner of a property vacats under their own free will.

50. Historical records of all previous owners and encumbrances of real estate is known as
    a. Chain of title
    b. Abstract of title
    c. History of title
    d. Title search

Answer: a. Chain of title

Explanation: The chain of title is a historical record of all encumbrances and previous owners to a specific piece of real property.

51. What is the easiest way to correct a cloud on a title?
    a. Abstract of title
    b. Chain of title
    c. Quiet title
    d. Create new title

Answer: c. Quiet title

Explanation: A suit to quiet title is a court procedure used to clear title disputes.

52. All of the following are required for a deed to be valid *except*
    a. Signature of the grantor
    b. Signature of the agents
    c. Signature of the grantee
    d. Legal Description

First Try

Answer: c. Signature of the grantee

Explanation: Signature of the grantee, legal description and consideration are all required for a valid deed.

53. Which of the following is typically prorated at closing?
    a. Property taxes
    b. Security deposits
    c. Administrative fees
    d. Employee costs

Answer: a. Property taxes

Explanation: Many states require their property taxes to be paid in arrears. Property taxes are typically prorated at closing.

54. Which clause in the deed conveys the rights and privileges of ownership?
    a. Acceleration clause

b. Deed clause

c. Right-of-use clause

d. Granting clause

Answer: d. Granting clause

Explanation: The granting clause in the deed conveys the rights and privileges of ownership.

55. What is the primary purpose of a title search?

    a. Establish proof that the seller has the right to sell
    b. Establish proof of address
    c. Determine any defects on title
    d. To transfer the deed

Answer: c. Determine any defects on title

Explanation: A property title search examines public records on the property to confirm the property's rightful legal owner. The title search should also reveal if there are any claims or liens on the property that could affect your purchase.

First Try

56. Which type of deed contains no express warranties?
    a. Warranty deed
    b. Bargain and sale deed
    c. Quitclaim deed
    d. Deed of trust

Answer: c. Quitclaim deed

Explanation: quitclaim deed gives the new owner whatever interest the current owner has in the property when the deed is signed and delivered. It makes no promises about whether the current owner has clear title to the property.

57. Title insurance protects against any title defect
    a. Found anytime
    b. Found before closing
    c. Found during the title search
    d. Found after closing

Answer: d. Found after closing

Explanation: The title commitment would list any defects found before closing and would exclude them from coverage, so only defects arising after closing are covered. A defect cleared by a quiet title suit is no longer a defect.

58. When a grantor signs a deed, what is the primary purpose of acknowledgment before a notary public?
    a. Show the grators signature was given without duress
    b. Required for transfer of ownership
    c. Prove the signatures were not forged
    d. Required by the lender

Answer: a. Show the grantors signature was given without duress

Explanation: If a grantor's signature was given while under duress, the deed is voidable.

First Try

59. In order for a deed to be valid, whose signature is required?
    a. Title company
    b. Grantee
    c. Grantor
    d. Both parties

Answer: c. Grantor

Explanation: In order for a deed to be considered valid, the grantor's signature is required.

60. When a lender agrees to accept property from an owner for less than the current principal balance on the outstanding loan is known as a
    a. Short sale
    b. Foreclosure
    c. Auction
    d. Lender buy back

Answer: a. Short sale

Greyson Roberts

Explanation: A short sale occurs when a homeowner in dire financial trouble sells their home for less than they owe on the mortgage.

General Real Estate Practice

61. For tax purposes, as a real estate salesperson, you're considered
    a. An employee
    b. An independent contractor
    c. A broker
    d. An LLC

Answer: b. An independent contractor
Explanation: As a real estate agent, you're an independent contractor whose income is solely reliant upon commission.

62. What type of tax document do you file as a real estate agent?
    a. W-2

First Try

       b. 1031
       c. 1099
       d. W-9

Answer: c. 1099

Explanation: As an agent, you're considered an independent contractor and will file a 1099 tax form.

63. How long would a party have to file a discrimination suit in federal court?
    a. 1 year
    b. 2 years
    c. 3 years
    d. Anytime

Answer: b. 2 years

Explanation: Parties must file a disrimination suit within 2 years of the event occurring.

64. A home for sale was marketed as a "good bachelor pad". Which statement is TRUE regarding this ad?
    a. Could be considered discriminatory
    b. This statement is totally fair game
    c. This is a good practice for marketing a smaller property
    d. Only bachelors should make an offer on the property

Answer: a. Could be considered discriminatory
Explanation: You should never advertise a property that is specific for a certain group of people. You may not discriminate against sex, race, familial status, religion, mental or physical disabilities or national origin.

65. A property is marketed as "55 plus" in a retirement community. Is this discriminatory?
    a. Yes, you may not discriminate against age
    b. No, retirement communities may discriminate against age
    c. Yes, FHA does not allow this

First Try

      d. No, you may discriminate against age

Answer: b. No, retirement communities may discriminate against age

Explanation: Title VIII of the Civil Rights Act of 1968, the Fair Housing Act, prohibits age discrimination in housing. A 1988 amendment to the act created an exemption for housing for adults age 55 and over as long as it provided facilities and services designed to meet the physical and social needs of the elderly.

66. Real estate broker commissions are negotiable when?
    a. Any time
    b. Only after closing
    c. Before closing
    d. Before an offer is made

Answer: a. Any time

Explanation: In real estate, almost everything is negotiable at any time until the property is closed, including agent and broker commissions.

67. What did the CAN-SPAM act establish guidelines for?
    a. Unsolicited cold calls
    b. Unsolicited text messages
    c. Unsolicited door knocking
    d. Unsolicited email messages

Answer: d. Unsolicited email messages

Explanation: The CAN-SPAM act established guidelines specifically for unsolicited emails.

68. "Those people are moving in down the street, you better sell now before they tank the value of your home!" This is an example of
    a. Redlining
    b. Blockbusting
    c. Steering

First Try

      d. Misrepresentation

Answer: b. Blockbusting

Explanation: The practice of persuading owners to sell property cheaply because of the fear of people of another race or class moving into the neighborhood.

69. Which of the following is an example of puffing?
    a. "This home has the best view in the neighborhood"
    b. Lying to a buyer about the financials of a property
    c. Misrepresenting the condition of the property
    d. Claiming a guaranteed return on investment of an income producing property

Answer: a. "This home has the best view in the neighborhood"
Explanation: Puffing is another word for exaggerating and is not illegal. Puffing should not be compared to misrepresentation and fraud.

70. "As an agent, I think that you won't like this neighborhood because of the ethnicities of the neighbors". This is an example of
    a. Blockbusting
    b. Redlining
    c. Puffing
    d. Steering

Answer: d. Steering

Explanation: the practice of persuading owners to buy a certain property in a certain neighborhood for reasons involving age, national origin, familial status, etc.

71. A lender denies an otherwise creditworthy borrower a loan because the lender does not like the neighborhood. This is an example of
    a. Blockbusting
    b. Redlining
    c. Puffing
    d. Steering

First Try

Answer: b. Redlining

Explanation: Redlining is the practice of denying a creditworthy applicant a loan for housing in a certain neighborhood even though the applicant may otherwise be eligible for the loan.

72. Which of the following do most states require on all real estate advertising?
    a. Salespersons phone number
    b. Salespersons address
    c. Brokerage firm's name
    d. Salespersons name

Answer: c. Brokerage firm's name

Explanation: In most states, law requires the brokerage firm's name on real estate advertising.

73. A broker uses a client's earnest money deposit to temporarily cover a business related lunch. Which of the following best describes this practice?
   a. Misrepresentation
   b. Commingling
   c. Perfectly legal
   d. Only legal if the broker replaces funds before closing

Answer: b. Commingling

Explanation: Commingling refers broadly to the mixing of funds belonging to one party with funds belonging to another party. It most often describes a fiduciary's improper mixing of their personal funds with funds belonging to a client.

74. In most brokerage firms, a salesperson compensation is most commonly
   a. A bi-weekly paycheck
   b. Commission-performance based
   c. A weekly paycheck
   d. A salary

First Try

Answer: b. Commission-performance based

Explanation: Real estate salespersons are most commonly compensated solely on real estate sales commissions.

75. When a broker hires an employee rather than an independent contractor, the broker is obligated to
    a. Withhold employment taxes
    b. Guarantee a schedule
    c. Not withhold employment taxes
    d. Provide commission compensation

Answer: a. Withhold employment taxes

Explanation: W-2 employers are required to without employment taxes from their employees paychecks.

Real estate math

76. As the listing agent, the seller agrees to pay 6% in agent fees, split between the buyer's agent and the listing agent. The sale price of the home was $100,000. What was the listing agent's commission?

   a. $6,000

   b. $3,000

   c. $1,000

   d. $10,000

Answer: b. $3,000

Explanation: $100k multiplied by 0.06 = $6,000. $6,000 divided by 2 is $3,000.

77. If the brokerage split was 70/30, what would the agent's commission be in the same scenario as stated in the previous question?

   a. $7,000

   b. $700

   c. $1,500

   d. $2,100

First Try

Answer: d. $2,100

Explanation: $100k multiplied by 0.06 = $6,000. $6,000 divided by 2 is $3,000. $3,000 multiplied by 0.7 is $2,100.

78. A commercial properties net operating income is $150,000. The fair market value of the property is $2M. What is the cap rate?

    a. 7
    b. 7.5
    c. 6
    d. 15

Answer: b. 7.5

Explanation: NOI divided by fair market value = cap rate. $150,000 divided by $2M is 0.075.

79. A property owner sold her home and paid 6% commission to the selling broker. If her net was $200,000, what was the sale price?

    a. $215,432

Greyson Roberts

      b. $203,758

      c. $600,000

      d. $212,765

Answer: d. $212,765

Explanation: 100% - 6% = 94% (sellers percentage). $200,000 divided by 0.94 = $212,765

80. A homeowner has a property valued at $125,000 that is assessed at 35% of its value. If the local tax rate is 6,400 mills per $100 of the assessed value, what are the monthly taxes?

      a. $233
      b. $245
      c. $236
      d. $145

Answer: a. $233

Explanation: Tax rate = 6,400 mills divided by 1,000 = 6.40 divided by 100 = 0.064 Assessed value = $125,000 multiplied by

First Try

35% (0.35) = $43,750. $43,750 multiplied by 0.064 = $2,800 annual tax. $2,800 divided by 12 = $233.33 monthly tax

81. An owner wants to receive a net of $82,000 after selling her home. She has an existing mortgage of $32,500 and will have selling expenses of $444. If the broker is to receive a 7% commission, what is the lowest offer that she can accept for the property?

   a. $121,473
   b. $122, 344
   c. $123,595
   d. $124,404

Answer: c. $123, 595

Explanation: The answer is $123,595.70. $82,000 + $32,500 + $444 = $114,944. $114,944 divided by 93% (0.93) = $123,595.70

82. If a seller's net was $255,000 after paying 6% in commissions, what was the sale price?

   a. $261,435
   b. $271, 276

Greyson Roberts

    c. $271,348

    d. $272,985

Answer: b. $271,276

Explanation: 100% - 6% = 94%. $255,000 divided by 0.94 = $271,276

83. If a 2,176 sq ft home sells for $118 per sq ft, how much did the home sell for?

    a. $217,600

    b. $255,768

    c. $281,391

    d. $256,768

Answer: $256,768

Explanation: 2,176 multiplied by 118 = $256,768

84. An apartment complex has a gross annual income of $125,000 and operating expenses of $65,000. What is the NOI?

First Try

      a. $60,000

      b. $125,000

      c. $190,000

      d. $65,000

Answer: a. $60,000

Explanation: $125,000 - $65,000 = $60,000 NOI

85. A borrower secured an $80,000 loan at 8.25% interest, and the lender's cash outflow was $77,600. What was the effective yield to the lender?

      a. 8.25

      b. 82.5

      c. 8.63

      d. 8.53

Answer: c. 8.63

Explanation: $80,000 – 77,600 = $2,400. 2,400 divided by $80,000 = 3 points (0.03). 0.125 multiplied by 3 = 0.375. 8.25% + 0.375 = 8.63%

86. An apartment complex has a semiannual income of $56,000 and appraised at $1,500,000. What is the cap rate?

    a.   5.64

    b.   7.46

    c.   8.41

    d.   6.46

Answer: b. 7.46

Explanation: $56,000 multiplied by 2 = $112,000. $112,000 divided by $1,500,000 = 0.0746

87. Two discount points cost a seller $2,000. What was the amount of the loan?

    a. $100,000

    b. $200,000

    c. $300,000

    d. $400,000

Answer: a. $100,000

First Try

Explanation: 1 discount point translates to 1% of the total loan amount. $2,000 divided by 0.02 = $100,000.

88. If the quarterly interest at 10.5% is $3,150, the principal amount of a loan is
    a. $105,000
    b. $131,150
    c. $110,000
    d. $120,000

Answer: d. $120,000

Explanation: To find the principal, divide the annual interest by the percent of interest. In this problem, to find the annual interest multiply the quarterly amount by 4. 4 multiplied by $3,150 = $12,500 (annual interest). $12,600 divided by 10.5% (0.105) = $120,000 (principal amount)

89. A buyer's agent closes on a property for $315,000. The seller is paying 6% in agent commissions split between the buyer's agent and the seller's agent. If

the agent representing the deal was a dual agent, what would their commission be?

    a. $18,900

    b. $18,100

    c. $17,900

    d. $17,100

Answer: a. $18,900

Explanation: A dual agent represents both sides of the deal. If the agent commissions were 6%, the dual agent receives all 6%. $315,000 multiplied by 0.06 = $18,900.

90. A lender agreed to a 90% loan-to-value (LTV) ratio with an interest rate of 8%. If the annual interest is $19,456, what was the loan amount?

    a. $245,399

    b. $234,200

    c. $243,200

    d. $235,200

Answer: c. $243,200

First Try

Explanation: $19,456 multiplied by 0.08 = $243,200.

91. A commercial property on the MLS is listed for $9/sqft/yr. The lease is for 3 years. What is the total cost of the lease if the property is 3,500 sqft?

   a. $84,500
   b. $94,500
   c. $93,400
   d. $35,000

Answer: b. $94,500

Explanation: $9 multiplied by 3,500 = $31,500. $31,500 multiplied by 3 = $94,500

92. Given the lease above, what would the buyer's agent commission be if they received 3%?

   a. $2,835
   b. $3,500
   c. $2,395
   d. $27,835

Answer: a. $2,385

Explanation: The commission is a percentage amount of the total lease amount. $94,500 multiplied by 3 = $2,835

93. A lender negotiated a $95,346 loan, which was 80% of the appraised value. The appraised value of the property is
    a. $119,125
    b. $119,182
    c. $118,374
    d. $120,125

Answer: b. $119,182

Explanation: $95,346 divided by 0.80 = $119,182

94. If a property's net operating income (NOI) is $36,000, and the property is valued at $300,000, what is its capitalization rate?
    a. 10

First Try

      b.   11

      c.   12

      d.   16

Answer: c. 12

Explanation: $36,000 divided by $300,000 = 0.12

95. If the cap rate is 5 and the property value is $530,000, what is the NOI?

      a. $12,500,000

      b. $10,200,000

      c. $10,600,000

      d. $5,300,000

Answer: c. $10,600,000

Explanation: $530,000 divided by 0.05 = $10,600,000

96. As the listing agent, you sold your clients home for $325,000 with 6% commission being split between the

buyer's and seller's agent. You are on a 60/40 with your brokerage. What is your take home commission?

    a. $8,450
    b. $5,850
    c. $3,250
    d. $6,100

Answer: b. $5,850

Explanation: $325,000 multiplied by 0.03 = $9,750. $9,750 multiplied by 0.60 = $5,850

97. If an interest payment of $1,500 is made every 3 months on a $50,000 loan, what is the interest rate?

    a. 9%
    b. 10%
    c. 14%
    d. 12%

Answer: d. 12%

First Try

Explanation: $1,500 multiplied by 4 (every 3 months is ¼ of a year) = $6,000 (the annual interest). $6,000 divided by $50,000 (the loan amount) = 12% (0.12)

98. An investor invests $20,000 into an income producing duplex. The pure monthly cash flow totals $450 per month per unit. What is the cash-on-cash return?

    a. 54%
    b. 20%
    c. 64%
    d. 25%

Answer: a. 54%

Explanation: $450 multiplied by 2 = $900. $900 multiplied by 12 = $10,800 in total yearly cash flow. $20,000 divided by $10,800 = 54% cash on cash return.

99. What is the estimated replacement cost of a 45ft. × 30 ft. building at an estimated cost of $141.50 per square foot?

Greyson Roberts

        a. $191,025

        b. $180,035

        c. $190,025

        d. $196,065

Answer: a. $191,025

Explanation: 45 multiplied by 30 = 1,350. 1,350 multiplied by $141.50 = $191.025

First Try

The big one

100. If you've enjoyed this book and you feel more prepared to tackle and pass your real estate exam on the first try, would you mind leaving a positive review on Amazon?
    a. Yes
    b. Yes
    c. Yes
    d. Eh, nope

Answer: d. Eh, nope

Explanation: You don't owe me anything. Just glad you enjoyed the book (although a review would be much appreciated!).

Chapter 8: Conclusion

There you have it! How to pass your real estate exam on the first try. Now, obviously you will need to understand many more vocab definitions as well as need to be able to pass many more practice exam questions than you went through in this book. I tried to give you the most entry level experience possible so it gives you a solid foundation to build your house of knowledge that you'll use to smash that test!

Real estate is a fantastic business and I wish you all the best success possible! Be sure to check out my youtube channel all about real estate at youtube.com/greysonroberts. Good luck!

First Try

Follow my real estate adventures on YouTube!

Scan me!

Made in the USA
Columbia, SC
26 September 2022